Strands of Time

Strands of Time

Selected Poems

For Kathy –
extraordinary woman –
enjoy!
Under Stohn

Johan Stohl

Dedication

This book is dedicated with love to Donna, my life-partner for over 55 years, and to our three children, Erik, Nathan, and Ingrid.

Cover photograph by the author

First edition printed November, 2014 by C-M Books, Ann Arbor, Michigan

Acknowledgements

I am grateful for the interest and support of those who have read and responded to my poetry over the years. I am especially grateful to Bill Gillham, longtime friend and former teaching colleague at Albion, for his ongoing encouragement, insights, and support.

For many years I have benefited from reading poems at the annual *Poetry Fest* held at Albion College in Albion, Michigan, and from several poetry readings held at Silver Maples in Chelsea, Michigan.

Special thanks to Katherine Hibbs, whose patience and editorial skills turned the manuscript into a publishable book of poems.

Foreword

Poets unfix the world…dwell in possibilities…
allow us to catch what we ordinarily miss.
(Brenda Wineapple, White Heat)

Poetry began and continues as an aural art
form, and like music is meant to be heard.
Whether a poem is read silently or aloud, we
often find ourselves *listening* to the rhythm of
lines and stanzas, the rhyming of words, the pace
and pattern of each poem. By the use of image,
metaphor, form and color, the language of poetry
invites us to *see* and *reimagine* reality through
our mind's eye, and to reflect upon the meaning
implied and expressed within each poem.

All of the poetry in this collection (including
Strands of Time) appears alphabetically by title.
The poems vary in length from those with just a
few lines to those that fill one or two pages. There
are poems on love, life, aging, death, time, nature,
philosophy and spirituality, as well as poems about
poetry itself, about what makes a poem, and how
a poem comes to be.

Contents

A Face So Fair

Would I could sculpt
a face so fair.

Now in her later years
she sleeps deep in
her favorite chair,
arms folded
feet raised high
head tilted to one side.

I could have cried
to see such
beauty
so at peace,
in bless'd repose.

A Poem's Progress

Some poems arrive like
morning dew…
fresh and
ready for review.

Some poems flow
like rushing
streams
and drown the
poet's nascent dreams.

Still other poems,
perhaps the
best,
progress much
like our human lives…
well-tempered over time,
redacted and
reworked
until each line
en route to the sublime
can find its own true rhythm,
quickening shape, and
final rhyme.

Abandoned

Before his execution...
feeling lost, alone, abandoned...
Meursault* finally achieved
a state of grace when
he accepted
and embraced the cold
benign indifference of the universe
toward his life and fate.

Surrounded by the beauty of
blue planet earth,
under a sky of stars
and moons, we too may feel
abandoned in the cosmic scheme of things...
but even nature's winds, floods, fires
volcanoes, earthquakes, storms
and rain cannot eradicate
the joy and pain
laughter and sorrow, that fills
our lives with meaning and desire,
connecting us to one another, and to those
saints we name and do not name
with whom we've lived
and loved.

(*Albert Camus, *The Stranger*)

Acceptance

Knowing that we're
going to die
someday
came home to me
when I was twelve, and
Grandma Cogswell passed away.

While everyone around her casket
stood and cried, I was
preoccupied
with peering in to see
if she still had her artificial eye . . .
the round glass eye that she
removed and dropped
into a water glass
beside her bed
when she lay down to nap each day,
after we had played our game
of anagrams.

Other deaths have come along . . .
parents, aunts, and uncles
cousins, nieces, nephews
and recently
too many friends.

And now I'm numbed
to hear
my sister dear
must deal with pancreatic cancer.

When Karin heard the news she
took it calmly, without fear
and seemed to be
as reconciled
to her fate
as fabled Sisyphus,
who stole the gift of fire
from the gods and was condemned
to roll his boulder up and down the hill
throughout eternity.

It's said he was content and
even happy with his fate,
and though my sister
feels sad that
life so soon will pass
she seems remarkably at peace
and ready to begin eternity
as she believes
within the mind God.

Acrobats

We watch the branches
move and
sway
high, high above,
where four-legg'd creatures leap
and play among the trees.

One acrobat creeps out upon
a willow bough that
bends so low
it seems
about to break.

With ten small fingers,
ten tiny toes, she
holds on tight,
her tail
swishing
back and forth…
balancing the way a
ballast steadies ships at sea.

From tree to tree these gymnasts
move around, up here, down there, while
holding fast with hands and feet,
then reaching out to make
another daring leap.

We love to watch them all day long,
running, jumping, scurrying
around high in the trees
and down here on
the ground,
the way all monkeys do.

So now, you see, we make our home
not in some warm and tropic land
but here in Michigan…
where every day
we see the squirrels chase and
play among the trees in our back yard.

Aerial Displays

Early one fine autumn day
we watch the throngs
of black-capped
chickadees
feed frantically
on sunflower seeds,
dive-bombing in-and-out
in splendid gay profusion.

Soon crowds of *nuthatches*
join in the churning turbulence,
creating with their graceful flight
fresh undulating patterns
in the morning light.

A vireo and several
tufted titmice soon appear
to feed on sunflower seeds.

Next, a *redhead woodpecker*
clings tightly to the
birdseed tray
while at the suet cage
a *downy* and its larger cousin *hairy*
thrust their beaks into the
seed-filled cakes.

Meanwhile a gentle *morning dove* pecks
all around for fallen seeds, and
raucous *blue jays* swoop on
down to take the corn
meant for our white-tailed deer.

Along the shore a rare *kingfisher*
eyes the shallow waters for
its morning meal…and
to our great delight
a lone *bald eagle* slowly
glides across the lake, its snow-white
head aglow, resplendent in the morning light,
casting far and wide for sunfish, perch,
and large-mouth bass.

Later that same day a great majestic shape
soars high above the marsh next to
our lake . . . it is the
great blue heron on mighty
wings, ascending stroke by stroke, then
turning back to glide and circle 'round…
an aerial ballet that spirals upward
and beyond to unknown regions
hidden far beyond, soon lost
within the dark blue sky.

Aesthetic Forms

It takes an artist's eye to see the hidden patterns
waiting every day for us to find.

One day we were amazed to see how Paul,
an artist friend, could take the
random scratches etched
in our canoe
and soon transform
them into rich aesthetic forms.

So when we seek more meaning in our lives
we will not stand around and wait like
Vladimir and Estragon,* hoping
"something will happen,
someone will come."

Instead we'll look within to
find some inner *mystic...poet...artist...*
ready to unlock our eyes,
unstop our ears,
and stir our
minds with unexpected new
designs, and unexplored connections.

(*From Samuel Beckett's Waiting for Godot)

Alone?

The silence of these infinite spaces strikes me with terror.
Blaise Pascal

Standing at the canyon's edge
under a perfect sky
the old eternal
question
echoes forth
from every side...
"Is anyone still there?"

At times we hear a haunting sound far
down within the canyon void,
reminding us we're
not alone...
for deep inside
the *rhizome of our souls*
we still can find the old abiding mysteries,
wherein we live and move and
have our being,
assuring us
we're not adrift upon
some dark, indifferent sea, but
anchored safely here, within
life's fearful symmetry.

Ambiguities

Lush ambiguities now fill each day
with illness, health, and energy
rich humor, curiosity
light comedy and
tragedy...
engaging hour-by-hour our
natural empathies and wider sympathies
whenever we connect with those
who share the passage
of our lives.

An Empty Chair

Several times each day I walk
or bike the trails that
loop around
the campground
here at Hunting Island...
a lovely off-shore barrier island near
Beaufort, South Carolina...and
every time I go around
I see an old man
sitting there
beside an empty chair.

He seems too frail to be there
all alone, but when I pass he nods at me
and waves his hand in greeting...and
once I stopped to talk, but he was
hard-of-hearing so I
moved on.

↘

Later I began to think about the
one I love back home.

Someday one of us will die,
and if it should be she
perhaps our
children will agree to
take me to a place like this, set up
my camp, and place two chairs there
side-by-side, where I can sit and
watch the passersby . . .
and say a word or
two before
we wave goodbye.

And then as others move along,
on down the road, my heart will ache
with longing for the one not
sitting there beside me.

An Open Heart

These songbirds sing
with lusty throats
wide open
on an August morn.

If we begin each day
with hearts so open, so attuned,
how can we fail to find the beauty
hidden deep within the souls of
those we meet along
life's way?

An Open Self

When we are
with a lifelong partner
or beloved friend
we need to
overcome our fears
and shed the armor that
protects our nakedness,
and put aside the veil
that hides us from
each other's
gaze...
and yet
let's not forget
that showing self to self may
put us on a path to being known
more as we are than as
we wish to be.

Aslant

Our aging lives
resemble late fall leaves
still clinging to the old oak tree
that grows beside our calm Mill Race...
a towering *axis mundi* of a tree,
huge-trunked with sprawling
arms and legs, a
Sumo wrestler
planted on the earth,
here in this sacred space.

Before dawn's early slant of light
these dusky dull oak
leaves, back-lit,
turn amber bright...
no longer old, but now aglow...
a wondrous sight.

Let us recall then as we age
that older lives, when viewed *aslant*
upon this bank and shoal of time
will soon begin to shine like
autumn's back-lit
leaves...and
glow as though transformed
alchemically into translucent gold.

At the Edge

Have you ever watched a caterpillar
inch its way across a tabletop,
then stop just at the edge
to stretch far out
and probe
the space beyond…
and when it finds there's
nothing there but air, it turns around
and quietly moves on?

Edges often mark the farthest end,
the terminus of things…
so when we
find we've gone too far
and reached an outer edge, we
usually turn around and seek another way.

While others hover near the edge
let us acquire
the *art of liminality*…
of dwelling on the threshold "here
and now" between time and eternity,
where we can stir the cauldron deep within
and learn to blend, as in a witch's brew,
life's vast complexity and
puzzling ambiguity.

At the Hermitage

–i–

We love these fields, these
rolling meadows and
winding trails
that lead us
deep into the woods
where we now sit and meditate
well-hidden from the herd
of white-tailed deer
who stand
nearby like
faithful brigadiers...
silent, alert, sensing our
presence, prepared to disappear
among the trees.

–ii–

Within this holy Hermitage
soft springtime breezes come and go,
the woodland life moves
to and fro...and
in these woods we know so well
songbirds begin to fill our souls with
warbling trills that flow from
deep inside their throats...

Oh how we're thrilled
by nature's singing minstrels!

Backlit

Our hearts awaken
with the morning light reflecting
off the tawny oaken leaves
that twist and swirl in
the wind like
opaque mirrors, or
Calder mobiles dangling from
the branches of the old oak trees.

Later in the day when
autumn light floods backward
through the trees, we find
these fading leaves
outlined as though
an artist's hand
had traced a laser
ray of light in soft embrace
around each dying leaf.

And soon our hearts again are stirred
when sunlight flows translucently
through all the changing
foliage of the leaves
that hang
from branches on
the nearby maple trees…

reminding us of magic lanterns all aglow
with yellow-greens and crimson-reds
and wondrous harvest-golds,
backlit and set
aflame in
many-colored splendor.

Now after all the years have passed
the beauty found within
our aging lives still
glows like
those fall maple leaves...
set-off, enriched and deepened
by the love and laughter, joy and pain
that's often seen, backlit and
burnished bright, inside
each living soul.

Balance Beam

Like gymnasts everywhere we make our way
along the balance beam of life, from
infancy to ripe old age,
enriched
each day by
wondrous mysteries
that fill and flood our souls with things
we've seen…and not quite seen,
truths known and still unknown,
poised always in-between
the two Infinities . . .
the macro world *without*,
the hidden micro world *within*.

And with each step along life's way we
find ourselves time and again
embraced
by *yin and yang*
with all its rich polarities
of life and death, of love and hate,
of will and destiny and fate.

And so our souls unfold through
darkest nights and
brightest days,
while deep inside we
find fresh intimations of *eternity*.

Bending Time

(an existentialist's dream)

We're told *the arc* of time
cannot be bent, nor
turned away
from its
appointed destiny,
nor curved to alter history.

Yet all *we now know of the past*
is but a finite single strand
selected from
the warp and woof
of streaming, endless time.

If what *has been* remains undone,
and *what's to be* not pre-ordained,
are we not free to
re-engage
through will and grace
the upward curve our lives will take
by shaping *what is past* and *what's to come*
in contours we desire and need
to realize our dream?

Benediction

We seek each day sufficient
time and breath to
reach the silent
spaces
deep within
where everyone
can rest and touch the
mystery of infinity... and
know wherein we live and
move and have our
being.

Beyond the Sorrow

Sorrow has its way with us...
it comes unbidden
to reside and
burrow deep inside,
then makes itself at home...
a sprawling, uninvited guest,
an octopus whose arms and tentacles
reach out to overwhelm our conscious minds
with an embrace that numbs our hearts
and souls with grief and
holds us fast...and
in the rhythm
of our loss
time and again
it comes to loose the
tide of unanticipated pain...
each time the same but not the same...
until at last sweet joy returns to
thaw the icy grip of grief,
unbind the hurt
around
our hearts, and heal
our wounds 'til we once more
can celebrate life's deepest mystery . . .
and savor now as ne'er before
the unbearable beauty
of Being.*

(*Milan Kandera's phrase)

Beyond This Shore

I sang in my chains like the sea.*
Captivity is Consciousness, so 's Liberty.**

–i–

Beneath the surface of our lives we are
sustained deep down
by taproots
reaching far below,
into the rhizome of our souls.

At night the tide of sleep
sets us adrift from
anchorage
that holds us fast by day
within the shallow waters of these
protective shores.

Asleep, adrift, we slip away from consciousness
and sail beyond our social sphere
into the vast
wide sea of dreams
where our poor, frightened selves
are free to laugh and cry and shake with fear
before the images and truths so
strange and dear that
draw us near.

–ii–

Haunted thus by night and day we've
learned to hide our dreams
away in memory
until asleep
we walk along that farther shore where
symbols have become our
native tongue,
infused with mystery.

And so upon that other bank
and shoal of time,
each night
we break the chains
that bind our hearts, and sing
the wildest songs our souls can sing
until this life is done.

*Dylan Thomas, Fern Hill
**Emily Dickinson, No Rack Can Torture Me

Blades of Grass

One day in early spring I sprawled
out on the lawn and stared into
a patch of grass, a tiny
forest filled with
subtle shades of green.

I viewed up close the way each leaf
grew from a tiny mound of earth,
each mound a small
volcanic cone,
and every cone packed full of
nutrient soil that fed the tender blades.

And as I gazed, transfixed and mesmerized,
each blade of grass, each size and
shape and shade of green,
appeared to me to be
as utterly unique
and singular
as human fingerprints,
or flakes of fallen snow.

Blowing in the Wind

Oh may we view
before the first of June
our Michigan woods bedecked in
Sherwood green, like Robin's merry band,
with tall cattails and prairie grass along each
country road, a-swaying in the breeze,
and wild springtime flowers astir
and glowing bright until
the summer ends.

Brother Ass

For eighty years dear Brother Ass has asked of me
a time for rest, a bed to sleep,
some food to eat…
and in return he's carried me
most faithfully upon his back, hither and yon…
not knowing whether, where or when
we'd end this wonderful
charade.

Buddha

Seated in full lotus position here
upon the ground, a beatific
smile upon his face,
his belly round,
the Buddha
finds in Nothingness
sufficient grace for being fully
present here-and-now within the swirling
rushing currents of this world…well
sheltered from the stream
of time by living now
within Eternity.

Common Ground

We woke to watch a
flock of bluebirds, finches,
chickadees flying around
with juncos on the
ground, all
seeking seeds
well-hidden now
beneath a fresh new
covering of snow that fell
all through the night, hiding
from sight the bird feed
we spread out upon
the lawn beneath
the snow.

And as the winter storm filled wood
and vale, a pure white blanket
spread across the land,
connecting all that
we could see
in perfect harmony.

I wonder if some day we'll
find a way to replicate
what Nature now
so naturally creates…
a common ground for all humanity?

Conclusion

In conclusion
let me say
our
human
all-too-human
ambiguous condition
serves us faithfully
and well.

Confused

As actors on the living stage
undone by Adam's fall
and caught
between the great and
small of Blaise Pascal's infinities…
those deep within, those out in space…
should we not seek both will and grace
that we might live courageously
within this age of moral
ambiguity?

Crocodile

O crocodile, that ancient smile . . .
Conrad Aiken

Not long ago a submerged log emerged
from deep within Lake Wintergreen,
exposing rows of broken spikes
along its back where
branches used
to grow, with two knotholes
where eyes might once have been.

And when we take our morning walk
along this quiet shore
we pass the spot
where hidden well within
the green-leafed lily pads the
crocodile waits patiently for unsuspecting prey.

So now we stay far, far away, up on the bank...
and as we stroll, we peer down at the
water's edge, wondering
when another hidden
reptile might
appear from deep
within this ancient glacial lake.

Dawn Doth Hover

Dawn doth hover at the break of day.
Soon consciousness will mount
a fresh assault upon
our dream-filled state and
scatter remnants of the night by
sending thoughts and sounds and sights
to shatter dreamy sleep, transporting
us away from this most wondrous
place between time
and eternity.

In our old age, as long as life
flows through these veins,
we hope to waken
every day
prepared to greet what
comes to meet us on life's way.

And once the sun has crossed the sky and
blessed nighttime has arrived
we'll shed the
remnants of the day,
retire, undress, and lie abed,
and wait for blissful sleep
to loft us far away.

Death Lingers

Death lingers in the air like
French perfume,
or like a
melody we've heard
that circles round and round
inside our minds, beyond our
grasp, just out of reach...
illusive, rare and
incomplete.

Deep Within

The way down is the way up.

–i–

At the bottom of these primordial lakes
exotic forms of life survive within
the watery depths…
while you and I
abide here on the shore,
skipping stones across the surface of our lives,
content to gaze out on the wave-filled surf
while we pursue our daily round of
ups and downs, afraid or
unaware of mysteries
deep within.

Is this to be our destiny…
to walk along
the water's edge, or
wander barefoot just offshore,
avoiding those realities that dwell
in darkness down inside
where we're afraid
to swim or dive?

–ii–
Throughout the springtime of our lives and
summer's long and languid days
we've lived our lives here
on the shore…
held back unconsciously it now appears
by circumstance and fear.

But gradually o'er many years our
fears began to disappear,
for we like
children everywhere
learned how to float and swim
and take deep breaths, and dive down
at the deeper end.

So now in these late passing years we're
not afraid to wade into
the foaming surf…
or swim far out until we
reach those greater depths where
unknown worlds await our final dives,
revealing wondrous mysteries
deep inside.

Dissonance

Be not dismayed to find in life
disturbing imperfections...
the subtle dissonance
within your
daily round, the
hidden sorrow found
within each joyous sound,
and deep in happiness
the quiet sadness
felt and known
whenever you're alone.

Dove's Death

I saw a
gentle mourning dove
struck down upon the lawn
beside our home.

All that remain are bloody
swirls in the snow where
feathers from her
breast now
mark the place
a wild hawk performed
its kill with swift unerring skill.

Survival governs nature's ways . . .
unlike Bin Laden or Hussein,
a hawk's most predatory
acts, like holy
sacraments,
serve only to preserve
the ordained scheme of things.

Downstream

Everyone lives downstream.
(Ecology bumper sticker)

Although it seems we live upstream,
we know that bits of gossip
quietly may float away
and later wash
ashore to
foul other souls, and ours.

We know that
just a touch of greed
though practiced surreptitiously
can spread throughout communities
the way a mold soon multiplies
its spores a hundred-fold
or more.

And might it be
that even minor venial sins
can bring the kind of suffering that
reaches far beyond ourselves,
and trashes other lives?

If such causality be so, we know
that thoughtful deeds
a kindly act
a loving heart expand
the circle of our lives, and
radiate like ripples on a lake or pond
to reach beyond into the
canyons of the soul,
and brighten
other lives that
share downstream our
dream of a redeemed humanity.

Dragonflies

Count them,
one...two...three...four...five...
sleek and slender
dragonflies
with needle-bodies
and fine-veined wings,
translucent as rare isinglass,
lined-up along our cottage deck in
perfect flight formation like
iridescent, bi-winged
fighter planes
arrayed
upon the decks
of aircraft carriers,
waiting for the semaphore
to launch them
one-by-one
upon another mission.

Are you and I, like dragonflies,
prepared to heed the
semaphore
that launches us
toward our final destiny
upon a distant shore?

Eve Was Framed

(a bumper sticker)

A bumper sticker once proclaimed
that Adam's mate should
not be blamed
for leading us astray.

'twas Eve as Mother of our race,
not Adam or the wily Snake,
who led us
out of Paradise
into this world of time and space…
enabling us to search and
find in human
history our
fate and destiny
while we embrace the
laughter, joy, and sometimes misery
that give to life its deep
rich ambiguity.

Ever and Again

We carry breakfast out onto
our backyard patio and
watch the morning
songbirds feed
while high
above
a steady stream
of yellow boat-shaped
cherry leaves takes flight.

They glide and float like
small canoes,
bobbing and rolling
on a restless tide of air
until they beach upon this shore,
where they'll be
reabsorbed
into the natural orb
of life and death and life,
ever and again.

Falling Leaves

Late last summer we watched
the wild cherry trees
that tower above
the maples
in our backyard
begin to lose their leaves.

They fluttered down like butterflies
in wild profusion upon the
rich green grass
beside our outdoor patio.

Soon a white-winged moth and
then a yellow butterfly
defied the pull of
gravity
and flew into the
cloud of falling leaves,
then disappeared among the
soaring cherry trees.

Festive Feast

The red-tailed hawk peers down but
cannot see the crested cardinal
bedecked in Chinese red,
resplendent in the
morning light,
concealed
behind a thick white
cloud of falling snow . . .
and when the heavy snowfall ends,
the songbird feeders that we fill each day
with thistle and black sunflower seeds for
bluebirds, finches, nuthatches, and
black-capped chickadees
will offer up a
festive feast
for birds of prey...
who must by instinct heed
the oldest law of nature still in play,
survival of the fittest.

Final Rest

Today I walked into the woods
behind our home until
I reached an old
oak tree,
then poured out on the ground
the powdery dust and fine bone fragments
from our parents' urns, tracing
a thin white line around
that towering
axis mundi of a tree
in memory of those whose lives
and last remains now lie forever blest
here in this hallowed
place of rest.

First Snowstorm

The first snowstorm arrived one late fall day,
a blinding shower of tiny pellets
driven slanting through
the morning air,
tearing away
the few remaining leaves
and sending them aswirl upon
the ground where they will fertilize the soil
in time for next Spring's Resurrection.

And at the entrance to these woods,
suspended from a low-hung
branch, the Big Ben
chimes swing
wildly...and improvise
a theme-and-variations of pure sound,
without a hint of melody.

Forever and Beyond

No matter where you stand, *infinity*
fills endless space here, there,
and far beyond.

No matter when you start, *eternity*
fills endless time now, then,
until forever.

Garden Buddha

Covered by a robe
with long and graceful folds
that sweep down from one shoulder
across his chest and thighs,
the marble garden
Buddha
sits in quiet inner peace,
and calmly captures in his lap
the sun and rain,
the wind
and falling leaves.

Throughout the years he sits
unmoved, untouched
by all the noise and fuss that
swirls around in endless wearying sound...
each day embracing in tranquility
the world's joys and pains
from deep within the
heart of Being.

Ghosts Don't Hide Outside

At night when I was very young I feared
the ghosts that lurked outside
my bedroom door...and
even when I closed
the door and pulled the shades
I knew that they could find a way to come inside.

But after years of keeping them at bay,
I realized one day that ghosts
and spirits do not hide
outside our walls, but here within.

So now we know there are no walls
to safely hide behind...and all
the things we fantasized
when we were young
dwelt not outside our minds
but here inside, as counterpoints
to deepen and enrich our lives each day
upon our way into old age.

Ghosts in the Machine

Cynics in this modern age
insist there is *no ghost in the machine…*
that we are bits of breathing matter
formed of nitrogen and calcium
of hydrogen and carbon,
along with other
elements…
and lots of water!

But do not you and I agree that
music, art and poetry
can stir and
summon forth
those hidden ghosts
that dwell in these machines
of bone and tissue, skin and sinew,
with synapses electrical,
whereby we
live and move and have our being?

Instead of *none*, or only *one*,
it seems
two ghosts now
dwell in these machines...
one fearful, grasping
trying to defend
itself
against the threats
and ravages of time...
the *other* more substantial ghost
transcendent,
full of life
and gratitude divine,
who leads us on to find some
holy place without . . . within . . .
where we can quiet life's noisy din
and revel in the *gift of being*
that comes our way
each day.

Halcyon Days

Early morning sunlight filters thru
these northern woods
creating random
patterns
on the
fern-filled forest floor.

Here I and my dear bride
of many years
retreat
to breathe the
deep and quiet peace
of good Lake Wintergreen...
while far away the
busy world of
politics and ideology
spins 'round and 'round.

We'll sojourn here awhile in Nature's Bower,
away from false theologies...and
breathe in every day
life's wondrous
mysteries,
filling our souls with
all the beauty we can find on
this small island, our haven
from the world.

Half-Lies

Hommage to political rhetoric

Malicious half-lies often flood our shores
through mental cracks and crevices,
the way Katrina breached the
shores of New Orleans,
filling unsuspecting
minds with
meretricious lies and
numbing all our faculties
before we realized it was too late
to renegotiate and then undo
the subtle damage
visited upon
our nation's soul.

If It Be True

If it be true as some have said that
"all the ancient gods are dead"
the rudder gone
the keel bent
the intervening
powers all fled, shall
we abandon faith, hope, love, and
leave behind a swirling wake
that drowns all deeper
higher states of
being?

'Ere it's too late let's
seek again in mystic space
the rich transcendent
warmth and grace
of nature's
dear
undying face...
with tracings of eternity.

Immortality Revisited

There is an inchworm
we've been told
that never
dies
but is
immortalized
year after year when
head and tail disappear and
new "ends" reappear.

And now it seems
(don't you agree) that
inchworms such as these
may live throughout
eternity.

But should this be
the only way to *immortality*
I would prefer to stay just as I am,
and keep things as they are at either end . . .

↘

unless somehow I find a way to spin my
own cocoon and in due time emerge,
the way a Lunar moth or
Monarch butterfly
creeps forth,
then soars aloft
in transcendental flight . . .
a fitting way to celebrate ones
mere mortality.

In Limbo
(after an operation)

Is it not time to take a break,
and undertake?

Profusion of
confusion reigns.

Perhaps some vast
inchoate plan prevails.

Awaiting fate
I linger in this limbo state
the body barely
breathing
nearly
stilled at last.

All work now done
let friends and lovers carry on.

In Memoriam

Banks of gray-white clouds
unfurl on a cold spring day like
billowing white-capped ocean waves
that race across a darkening sea..
and all our thoughts and feelings
churn and swirl inside this wild
tsunami of mortality.

Recently a friend of ours
died unexpectedly
and for a time
the thawing season
in our souls will be on hold
'til knowledge of that death finds rest
within the hidden sanctuary
of our lives.

And when in time the time is found
for us to come again into our
normal daily round
we will rejoin all those who
live and move and share their being within
the beauty of this unique community
we now call home.

In Such Uncertain Times

In such uncertain times as these
when we're
undone by news
that's hard to bear, and
find our minds o'erwhelmed with
mingled hopes and fears,
let us return and
hear again
those melodies
from early years that
filled our ears with transcendental
music of the spheres.

In the Mirror

What we *think* we see
here in the mirror
may not be
here…or there…
for we have changed
in many ways over the years
and may not see
the change,
or seeing, not believe.

Once upon a time when
we looked in
the looking glass
we *were* the Princess dear,
the handsome Prince,
besotted by
our younger self, not
knowing who or what we were.

But now it's time to let fair Beauty
sleep…she's had her day,
her way with us, and
we are just
as we should be,
of an uncertain age,
old, wrinkled, slow of speech
with halting feet, no
longer filled
with foolish vanity, but
wise and aging gracefully.

Incandescence

Incandescent
in her coat of many colors
like a lovely stained glass window
her beauty now at seventy-nine
remains undimmed
by time.

Infinity

The silence of these infinite spaces strikes me with terror. Blaise Pascal

–i–

In early fall before
the trees begin to lose their leaves
the woods appear dense
dark and deep.

But when the leaves have fallen from
the plants and shrubs
and trees
we gaze into
these finite woods,
late in the fall, and find
they are not deep
at all.

–ii–

At night, ten thousand stars light up the sky,
but they appear to be far out of reach
until we use a
telescope to peek
into the deep night sky,
past all the stars, beyond our galaxy,
into the vast dark distant space
we like to call Infinity.

Intermission

Between the rain and early dawn...
after the night has come
and gone...we lie
abed and tell our dreams,
and watch the deer out in the woods
leap single-file through shrubs and trees,
their heads and white-flag tails
held high, alert to every
subtle sign of
danger.

Now songbirds
waken and arrive to feed
on our black sunflower seeds while
we two sleepy-heads remain
just where we are and
want to be...
refreshed by last
night's restful sleep, not
ready yet to terminate this
quiet intermission.

Is It Not Time?

–i–

We're told it's time to put aside bell,
book, and candle burning,
for chemists find
in bread and wine
no sacramental churning,
and yeastless bread with holy wine
arouse no spiritual stirring.

So shall we then abandon all our
ancient ritualizing, and live as
modern women and men
devoid of higher
learning…
no longer seeking
higher truths through
transcendental training,
content to live *sans sacrament*
and deeper spiritual
meaning?

And when at last that day arrives and
we prepare for dying, can
we be sure there
is no hell,
no unrequited yearning?

Since specters of an afterlife by
now have grown passé,
and many age-old
ritual-myths
no longer are in play,
let us not try to hedge our bets
against some distant day, nor
seek to hide our soul's
desire to
find another way.

And now we know this modern age
of false and arid piety creates a
longing and a need for
holy mystery that
we now satisfy
each day
thru music, art and poetry.

Is There a Ghost?

Is there a ghost in these machines, some
unseen *immaterial presence*,
a *mind or soul*
that finds itself at home within
this house of muscle, ligament and bone . . .

a mind sustained by blood and oxygen
that seeks to find a way to know
the timeless truths that stir
below the surface of
our lives, day after day . . .

a soul that dwells down deep inside,
beside the sacred *axis mundi*,
the hidden tree that
grows and
thrives
well-rooted at the
center of each being?

And so again we ask,
is there a ghost in this machine,
some *haunting presence*,
some *mind or soul*
that sets us free
to ponder and explore life's mysteries...
lest we should go astray, and drift
away into a mindless sleep?

Lace Curtains

A pair of old lace curtains,
frayed and threadbare
after years
of wear,
translucent in
the morning light
and printed here and there
with images of birds in flight
swirls through an open
window in
Andrew Wyeth's
painting, *Wind from the Sea.*

It seems the artist is aware
of all the weary
loneliness
and fear
we fail to observe
inside that room behind
the restless frayed-edge curtains
that blow and wrap
about the old
unpainted window frame.

↘

Outside the land unfolds across
an open field that leads
into the woods,
while deep
within our lives truths
lie in wait, like those concealed
behind this careworn pair
of old lace curtains.

Lake Wintergreen Retreat

Last night we watched as fireflies
flew back and forth
across the lawn,
flashing
on-and-off,
off-and-on...and with
the coming of the dawn,
a thousand tiny points of light
appeared and disappeared
like diamonds riding
on the waves,
rippling o'er
the sunlit lake below.

This jewel of a lake took shape
ten thousand years ago
when glaciers
entered from the north, and
in retreat embedded footprints in the earth...
huge craters that became a hundred
glacial lakes, each with
a special name like
"Wintergreen,"
so-named because along its shore
wild berries grow...tender, ripe, and sweet.

↘

Tonight we'll gaze up at the moon,
then at the waters down below
where soft moonlight will
flood the lake
with ghostly
forms and shapes
reflected from the fluffy clouds above,
inviting us to find what's hidden
deep within our minds
before we
fall asleep here at
our blessed dome retreat.

Let Holiness Abound

Why must we seek to understand
the simple mysteries that
come and go...the
daily miracles
we find in
nature all around,
and in our life together?

Each day can we not let the sense
of *wonder* have free play,
unclaimed by ideology
that stifles and
obscures
each day's epiphanies?

Oh let us let
true holiness abound by
diving down, deep down into
our lives, that we might
know transcendence
in the daily round
of living
here and now...
'til death takes us away.

Life's Tapestry

Dare we be free enough to own the past...
and fashion for ourselves a
true life history?

As decades pass, we seek to grasp
from time to time
within our minds some
sense of life's rich treasury
by joining what is past and present
with what is yet to be . . .

And after years of joyful
painful
divings deep
into those long past days
we pray at last the time arrives
when we can comprehend and blend the
passing years and years to come
into a bold rich tapestry of
gratitude and praise.

Mendacity

Like carrion and buzzing flies
our politics and public
lies pollute the
very air we breathe,
divert, mislead and trivialize the
serious issues of the day 'til
we are all betrayed
and left not
knowing
whether/what
we should believe.

When lies control politics we lose all
sense of what is true, distort
the common good
and break the trust
that binds us one to one...
for once the lie becomes the truth
distrust appears and leaves
us ripe for tyranny.

Then must not justice, love and truth
become as golden threads that
bind us day-by-day to
our democracy
by shaping what we
think and do, believe and say...
and deepening our
humanity?

Metamorphosis

A patch of melting ice
refracts the morning light,
creating rare and random
patterns captured by the
camera's macro lens,
revealing Nature's
rich variety
in silent imagery.

Every close-up is a
subtle masterpiece of
chiaroscuro, light and dark,
upon the frosted window panes
that frame our lovely northern woods...
while down the hill, the frozen
hibernating lake begins
its springtime thaw
too late.

Mind of God

We're told that when we die our physical reality
reverts from matter into energy.

As physicists now theorize,
within our universe
material things
compress inside black holes . . .
and all we've been and known and loved,
our friends and family,
our work and play and creativity,
our transcendental days of
simple joy and ecstasy
will be encoded
two-dimensionally
within a "membrane"
that absorbs/preserves reality
next to the edge of some black hole
in such a way that it can later
be restored to three
dimensionality.

↘

It's also claimed that
time is not a flowing stream
that moves from past to present
into some new and future time
but rather, like a
frozen pond,
time doth comprise what
was, and is, and will yet be
within this moment,
presently.

If this be so is it not like the *Mind of God*
wherein it's said "we live, and move
and have our being . . ."
a *Mind* that holds
enduringly
all that we are and
were and ever hope to be...
throughout Eternity?

Mothers and Daughters

Mothers and daughters find
their lives enriched
by ambiguities
that
over time
bind them more
deeply, freely to each other.

As years go by they
try to probe and
understand
the subtle precious
strands and threads that
wind all through their lives,
binding their hearts
in love.

Mowing Grass

After the rain
he mowed the lawn in
flowing patterns
round and
round,
front to rear,
never stopping,
backing-up or taking
sharp right-angled turns,
and leaving in his wake a
lovely patchwork quilt
imprinted on the
grass.

Muse

If ever again I must contend
with words and images
that fill my
unsuspecting brain, then
only then will I seek out the Muse
whom once I promised and agreed to heed
should I again be made to feel her
inconvenient stirrings
deep within.

My Father's Words

"Habit is a wonderful thing"
he said...but I forgot
his words the
way I often did
when what he said
slid down inside my mind,
as though transplanted underground
like bulbs buried deep
and out of sight
where they lie dormant
'til a springtime thaw arrives,
and it is time to bloom again...
tho' not too soon.

Years after he was laid to rest
my father's voice
returned
in perfect rhythm with
the seasons of my soul . . .
and once again I heard his words
as echoes from long, long ago
when I was far too
young to know
what simple wisdom
hidden deep inside might
lie in wait, and then emerge
on such a day as this, just when a
springtime thaw was due.

Naming Is Not Knowing

If names and dates and places
start to stick inside my mind
from time to time
like flies
to fly paper,
I would not mind.

Sometimes I'm asked, "Now what is
that familiar piece? Is it by Brahms
or Debussy?" as though
by naming
(could it be) the
poetry is better known...
the music far more heavenly.

For those who ask, the names affixed
to music, art, and poetry
adhere like Velcro
in their minds,
and are recalled with
ease...or so it seems to me.

↘

While they remember every name
I'm swept away
by wondrous sounds
that swirl around within my brain . . .
and I am ready now to lead each
voice and instrument into
such warm rich
harmonies
of rhythm, pace, tonality
that all who hear may soon be
drawn into the wondrous
dance of life.

Nature's Epiphanies

Why don't we stop and rest this late fall day
beside these lovely woods
with all their beauty
on display,
surrendering to
the wonderful parade . . .
the fleeting, passing panoply of
leafy crimson...auburn...rust and gold...
and rich deep ochre blended-in...
along with many shades
of green.

Are we too bound by time
to pause before such autumn beauty,
knowing as we do that all too soon
these woods will lose their
leafy glow and
soon appear
cold and forlorn, like
stiff and naked skeletons or
stoic sentinels, proud and erect,
enduring winter's fierce
and hoary blasts.

↘

It's sad we cannot shake the
chains of time and
stay awhile to
enjoy this natural beauty.

Indeed sometimes I envy Sisyphus…
his body chained eternally,
his mind set free,
discovering
every day a new epiphany.

Now and Again

While songbirds flock to feed
on sunflower seeds in
our backyard,
high
high above a
steady stream of boat-shaped
ochre cherry leaves takes flight.

They float and glide and dip
down through the air
like small canoes
upon a
restless sea, bobbing
and rolling as they descend...
until they beach upon the forest floor
where they'll be reabsorbed into the
natural orb of life and death
and life again, until
life's final end.

Odyssey of a Soul

(Synopsis of Dante's Divine Comedy in 1300)

By nature's alchemy the
world moves from springtime greenery
through summer's heat and wild growth
and autumn's golden finery
before descending into
winter's icy cold.

Now in this winter of our discontent
we must descend to
mystic depths
by diving once again
down into Dante's *Divine Comedy*.

And thus with Virgil as our guide
we're led into the vast
Infernal regions
of the soul,
where sin and misery abide.

From thence with hopeful upward stride,
we enter *Purgatorio*, where we
must struggle and repent
until well-shriven
and forgiven
we find ourselves before
the golden gates of *Paradiso*.

Here Sainted Beatrice soon arrives
to take us by the hand and
lead us far beyond
what we
unaided could attain
with our imperfect wisdom...
for we are overwhelmed and lost
without her mystic
radiant vision.

And now at last
we find ourselves in *Paradise*
where still we stand, amazed and
dazed, in utter silence...
gazing out upon
the wondrous presence of divinity,
renewed, transformed and baptized yet again
into that pure unending
Sea of Love.

Old Wood Bench

Like a dear friend the wooden
bench sits all alone
next to the
woods,
where people
on the Wellness Path
can rest and watch the men
pitch horseshoes from each end.

Today the bench has disappeared,
the horseshoes put away,
and as we gaze into
the woods
we view the naked trees
shorn of their oak and maple leaves…
and sense the absence of the old wood bench,
vanished as though by thieves at night,
or hidden out of sight.

Through winter's clime we are content
to stay inside and listen to our
woodland chimes,
and watch as
squirrels, deer, and hares
forage among the woodlands bare,
'til winter's gone, and
spring arrives,
and leaves appear upon
the trees, and songbirds fill the air.

After the bench has reappeared
and older men begin again
to pitch their shoes,
we'll take a seat
out on the old wood bench,
and watch as iron shoes fly by, and
listen for the ringing peal of
steel-on-steel
as horseshoes clang
against the iron posts and
strike against each other…then
thud upon the ground.

On Poetry

If we attend to poetry the way we
listen to a symphony
or view
creative works of art
we'll soon begin to grasp
and then appreciate the rich intensity
of language chosen for our ears...
for poetry is meant
for us to hear,
and if we cannot hear it
read aloud, it can be heard
and listened to inside
our minds while
we sit quietly alone.

And so when reading silently, let's
listen for each subtle nuance,
shift in rhythm,
and hidden rhyme
as line-by-line we take delight
in language used to alter mood
and tone and pace,
that we might come in time
to understand what poetry can mean
and be...and bring reality
into our lives.

On Writing Poetry

It seems to me that bit by bit
a poem comes to be
by conjuring
words and images
as offerings to an unknown deity.

Gradually a form takes shape
as content, rhythm,
rhyme come
consciously to mind.

Once written down, the fuss begins—
a change of word, a phrase replaced,
whole stanzas altered
swapped, erased.

At last I'm ready to let go and
read the poem aloud.

"I like it," Donna says. A pause.
"Have you . . . ? Could you . . .?" A longer pause.
"And what about the way it ends?"

I cringe and say aloud (too loud),
"It's *right* the way it is!" —
a phony ruse, for
though I know the poem
needs more work, more time,
it is too young, too tender now
to be redone . . .

↘

But like a hound, I cannot leave the poem alone
and in an hour, more or less, I'm back
again to gnaw that bone.

Writing a poem gives little rest...and
yet, as in a state of grace,
one feels blessed

Open Hearts

While songbirds sing
with lusty throats
wide open
on this
August morn
dare we begin our day
with hearts so open, voices so *attuned*
we cannot help but see the
beauty hidden deep
within the souls
of those we
meet along life's way?

Opposites

A shadow cuts across my mind,
dividing light from dark and
life from death, for
I have just remembered
that a much-loved colleague
will be "laid to rest" this afternoon
at St. James Church.

Hindus say that
opposites do not exist...
that they are just the play of *maya**
messing with our minds until
we find enlightenment...
and all these
separating opposites
that so divide our minds
like "true and false" or
"right and wrong"
are rich polarities...
the common *yins and yangs* of life
that round the circle of our days and
set aright the *symmetry* of dark and light
to aid us on our upward flight
into eternity.

(*The world as known through our five senses)

Orange Guitar

He *drew* a wondrous
orange guitar
with squares
of blue on bluish jars...
his gaze affixed on things afar...
creating rare sounds
strange and true,
pure music
flowing
old and new
soft, sad and blue.

Now people come from
near and far to
hear him
play
his orange guitar.

Parallel Lives

Emerging from a common root
like Siamese twins
this maple tree
contains
two trunks
paired side-by-side,
entwined in close embrace
along their upward climb . . . the way
young lovers often cling,
bound close to one
another like
double helix strands of DNA.

But when two try to live as "of one flesh"
their tenderness may not o'ercome
the test of close communion...
and so in time
they find those roots that
once held them so close begin to
lose their hold until they are
no longer bound by
deeper ties, and
soon live parallel lives...
resigned to dwelling side-by-side as
former lovers but still friends
who seek to find another
life and destiny.

Parallel Worlds

Sometimes I see how far apart
we live our lives from art.

–i–
During an exhibit of Van Gogh's art,
we watched two boys pass by his
painting of a pair of boots.

As he walked by, the first boy chattered on about
the artist's skill, his choice of subject,
brush strokes, color, style . . .

The second boy stood quietly before
the painting, then cried out, "*Mommy,*
whose boots are *those?*"

–ii–
It seems as though
an artist's rendering unveils
deeper meanings and conditions,
offering parallel dimensions
that can seep into our
well-constructed
view of things,
upsetting our convictions and
enriching our perceptions by revealing what is
true and good and beautiful...
and even everlasting.

↘

–iii–

A literature professor told his class he
hoped the time would come
when each of us would
learn to
"read the world"
through images from fiction,
trusting our imaginations to reveal
how everyday reality is but a shadow of
the truth we find in drama, poetry and art.

Some years later I remember seeing a young
woman walking down a city street
and knew immediately that
she was Dreiser's
Sister Carrie.

Patterns

Songbirds flying here and there
through empty space
trace undulating
patterns in the morning air.

Ballerinas of every size and age
move out upon the
practice floor,
leaping, pointing, shaping
fine-tuned bodies into contoured
graceful silhouettes.

Sculptors slowly carve from
blocks of marble the
silent hidden
forms
that wait within
their mute white stones,
uncovering new and rare
designs invisible to
our naked
untrained eyes.

Pileated Wonder

Like *déjà vu* all over he's back again, this
Ichabod Crane with wings, this lean
lank scarecrow of a bird.

Loud pecking sounds
resound whenever
he strikes
wood,
his hammerhead
relentless, without pain
through some genetic evolutionary fix
of sinew, nerve and bone.

Fierce-eyed he stares,
bold, stark,
unblinking, with a
rakish head, red-tufted…and
whenever he flies by, patches of white
are visible beneath his wings, a
fearful prehistoric sight.

Unlike this Pileated one, the
legendary *Ivory-billed*
evokes no fear
when it is near...for
like the *Redhead, Hairy, Downy,*
Flicker, and *Red-bellied* too,
it seems to be a tame
domesticated bird
compared
to this epiphany of
ancient symmetry found here
within the Pleated woodpecker that
owns and rules the woods
around our Dome.

Pink Flower Petal

A pink flower petal
shaped like a tiny kite
with variegated
veins and
light green accents
along its stem and outer edges
floats curled-up here on its back
in a clear glass of water.

No longer fed and kept
alive connected to
its mother plant,
if it's to die
I'd rather
see it floating
on a rushing stream,
or tumbling over waterfalls,
or braving rapids 'til its trapped
within a whirlpool where it will
circle round-and-round, then
like our human lives
swirl down into
eternity.

Press of Time

Day by day the wild whirligig of life
engulfs our hearts and minds
with stressful signs.

Should we not seek then every day
to *stay* the press of time…
suspend the
ordinary flow and
slowly age like fine French wine?

When we were in our salad days, or
vigorous in our middle years,
we sallied forth like
gallant knights
to fight all foes and right all wrongs.

Now past our prime my dear
we're at a time when
we should dine on
finer things…
a Galway flute,
or Van Gogh's boots,
or Mozart's glorious Requiem…
for beauty brings forgotten feelings forth
to heal and cleanse our troubled
minds, and flood our souls
from deep inside with
fresh epiphanies.

Pruning

Yesterday's strong cleansing winds
trimmed from the trees their
leaves and limbs,
and littered
our back yard
before we raked it clean.

Our souls often need such winds to
trim away the waste and sin
which we then rake
into a pile
and set afire…
that grace might enter in.

Quiescent Muse

The Muse remains quiescent, lying
silently in wait, just
out of sight...
a Tiger burning
bright, prepared to strike.

Quiet Waters

The way
great ocean waves
find time for quiet calm
reminds us we too
need to find
some
quiet time
to quench our
thirsty souls in soundless
depths deep down...
lest we should
drown.

Rain of Petals

We watched as clouds
of small white
petals
rained down
upon the ground,
like shining drops of light...
a hundred thousand snow white blossoms
descending in a shower of fragrant
flowers, shimmering bright
against the
darkened woods beyond,
where branches swayed and springtime
leaves spun round and round,
driven by the swirling
wind...and then the
Big Ben chimes,
stirred by the breeze,
joined in to help us celebrate this
lovely springtime shower.

Red Balloon

Do you remember watching as
the red balloon
slipped from a child's hand
and floated upward toward the sky . . .
and grownups tried in vain to catch
the tethering string before
it flew away?

One night we met some friends at *LIVE*,
near downtown Ann Arbor, to hear
Dapogny's big band sound…
and while we sat,
off to one side
a figure caught our eye,
a single girl dancing all alone.

She was an ingénue, half-woman, half-child,
wearing a peasant blouse and
thread-bare jeans, a
solitary dancer lost
within her private world.

Drawn by her
simple grace and charm
from time to time some of the older
men would ask our *ingénue* to dance . . .
and though she joined them in the
rhythm of the band, she moved
as though she danced
alone, attuned
to some
mysterious inner world.

All evening long it was as though
her feet were inches
off the ground...
a winsome waif, afloat on air,
free and untethered like a red balloon.

Restive Muse

A restive muse insists on
having her own way with me,
gently at first with
words, ideas,
images
astir in my
unconscious mind, but
when I fail to heed her call
she makes me pay with interruptive
thoughts and promptings through the
day, until I once again agree
to play her game.

Seaweed

Medusa must have strolled these
ancient shores and spread her
wild, serpentine hair
like strings of
seaweed
all along the
sandy beach, adorning
driftwood, sea shells, jagged rocks
and clam-clogged furrows
burrowed in the sand.

Gnarled, knotted, strung with
bulbous beads,
this ancient seaweed
comes to life each day, watered by
the rising tides of Fundy Bay.

And as each tide recedes,
her tangled hair fair glistens in
the morning sun, glowing
an iridescent green
upon the sand…
while far out from the land
we spy a blue-green hue reflecting
off the surface of the Bay,
and wonder what
exotic life is living there
deep down, that we will never
know or understand.

Shape Shifting

−i−

Dark shadows move
across the lawn
beneath the swaying trees
like shifting Rorschach blots of ink,
changing so rapidly
we find it hard to
recognize a
shape,
detect a form,
conjure a name.

−ii−

Every day in Plato's Cave
a hundred thousand
images
flash across the
crowded screens of our poor brains,
confusing sense with essence
form with substance…
conjuring us to
capture and hold fast
to old and fixed ideas that
morph inside our minds.

–iii–
Such is the work of Maya
who every day creates beguiling
shapes and shades
that lead us
far away from
what is real and true,
seducing us with subtle shifting images
and fleeting shadows that beguile our five senses,
sight and sound, along with touch and
taste and smell, until we lose our
way back to reality.

Sheltered Lives

Creeping up and down the deep, deep
corridors of time, we find
these ancient
turtles
still alive on every
wind-swept sandy beach.

Protected by their hard-shelled homes
they live for years until the
time arrives when
they and we
will be transformed
into another living form.

And like surviving turtles with their shells
we hope that we'll continue
in old age to wander
and explore...
and probe life's deeper
mysteries before we've grown
too old to know,
or care.

Six Swans

One morning we awoke here at the Dome
to witness six white swans out on
the calm and quiet waters
of Lake Wintergreen.

The sun glowed fair
upon their snow-white purity,
and we were stunned to silence
by the radiant display
of rich unearthly
beauty
rarely found in
nature's vast unfolding panoply.

Now after thirty years up north
without a trace, how
can it be that
six white swans should
suddenly appear here on
an autumn day in such
a brilliant rare
epiphany
upon this lake
created long ago,
when glaciers scouring deep
disfigured earth's old face and left
behind this heavenly place...
these lovely woods and
ancient lake.

Solitary Leaf

A solitary leaf clings to an
old oak branch long
after other trees
have lost their leaves.

Each day we watch its
brave display
of leafy acrobatics...
somersaults and pirouettes
and spinnings round and round,
the way the winds of fate
by which we're
bound play
freely with our lives.

And every day we waken to the way
our lives, propelled by will
and grace, lead to
a common destiny...for
on some future unknown day
we'll be set free, and like a solitary leaf
fall to the ground and disappear
without a trace, earth to earth
ashes to ashes, dust
to dust.

Yet might it be
our souls will soar
beyond this time and place
into a parallel universe,
where we'll be
face-to-face
with life's great mysteries?

Solstice Day

During the longest night of every
year we seek the darkness
down inside that
germinates
new forms of life from
seeds of truth and beauty buried
deep within.

Now on this Solstice Day
we pray that fresh
epiphanies of
rarest roses, sharpest thorns
will blossom forth in wild and riotous
display, out of the fertile
rhizome of our souls.

Solstice Night

No longer do we need the ancient
tales and myths to lead us
fathoms deep
into the dark night
of the soul, where in the
shadowed light of consciousness
we waken to the revelations
of a solstice night.

So let the morning light not soon
displace the dark of night...
for if that light
arrives too soon, it
will reveal and then betray
the living myths and truths that lie
concealed beneath the daytime
masks that we remove...
hoping we might
learn anew
just who we really are on
this, the darkest night of all the year.

Someday

It would be sweet
if we could
meet
again
some day
when time is
measured by Eternity.

Something in the Air

A tomb is not a place to stay...but
who will roll the Stone away?

Something in the Easter air
doth stir our
spirits fair, for we must
meditate on deeper things...
the flaming chalice,
the bread and
wine...
reminding us
of that great myth,
when all mankind was
sanctified upon a Cross,
and time symbolically
was bound for
all eternity
by vines of pain
and crowns of thorns . . .
the very mystery embodied deep
within each springtime rose.

Special Day

As clouds pass by
and morning sun arrives
and all the darkened woods
are dappled bright
with light,
deep
deep within
I feel again the way
I felt on Christmas Day when
we crept softly down the stairs,
amazed to find the tree
lights all ablaze.

Spider's Web

Spun from within, a spider's web becomes
a sheer transparent lair wherein
arachnids snare their
unsuspecting prey
with sticky filaments that
hang suspended in the air . . .
each web an architectural miracle
beyond compare...and though
such webs cause many
deaths, they're
also lovely
gossamer things that
serve as metaphors for those
resilient human cords spun deep
within our souls that bind us one to one,
day after day, within the human family
in which we live and move and
have our being, part of the
wondrous web of life.

Stolen Moments

I like to steal moments in between
uneven beatings of my heart...
when every hour turns
fresh and green
with promises
of days to be, and we
are free to journey on our way.

Strands of Time

Frayed at both ends
the silver strands
of time
like twine
unwind, unravel and
contend with grief and loss,
with pain and death,
'til all that's left
as evidence,
as concrescence,
is timeless presence
of *Eternity*.

Stung By a Bee

Stung by Eternity
or a Bee
leaves
a stinger
deep in me.

Surely the Gods

On Puerto Rico's southern shore
we stopped at whimsical
Mary Lee's to
rent *Pacifica by the Sea.*

Here pelicans soar up high and dive,
while geckos dart along
the walls,
and scrawny
roosters crow at dawn,
their raucous calls resounding
all around the land.

One day we found our way
to Casse Grande...
a lush moist
mountain hide-away,
a sacred place with evening mists
fresh morning dew
a brilliant sun
rare clouds, soft rain, and
dark green red-tipped flowers
that adorn each hill like precious lace.

"Surely," we say, "the gods must dwell
within this holy place."

Tenderness and Truth

Tenderness and truth lie only in the depths . . .
*everything above is harsh and false.**

Do we believe our hearts to be
so cold and ego-bound
they must remain
imprisoned
in these shadow lands, like
prisoners chained to Plato's Cave?

Is truth too deep, too well-disguised
for us mere mortals to unmask
its many masquerades,
and set it free?

Through music, art and poetry
let us enrich our lives
with such deep
truth and tenderness that
our poor souls will sing in ecstasy.

*The last words from Wagner's *Das Rheingold*,
sung by the Rhine maidens.

Thud

Yesterday we heard a thud
against our patio door
and with a sense of dread we
went to find a house finch lying there,
unmoving, stunned and dazed...or
dead...upon the patio floor.

At first we felt compelled
to pick it up
and see if its small
heart was beating still,
but since we knew we ought
to give it time
alone
we went away . . .
and later we returned
to find the injured bird alive and
creeping on the ground outside the door,
before it disappeared.

Sometimes we find a songbird
lying there, and later we
return to see
the bird has gone, and
always wonder if it flew away...or
if a feral cat or hawk came scavenging that day.

↘

Now when we find a songbird
lying motionless, its heart
not beating,
feathers stilled...
unmoving and unmoved...
we carry it into the woods and
find a place of rest where it can be
transformed, in time, by
nature's alchemy...
ashes to ashes, dust to
dust, into life's final mystery.

Twisted Trunk

At Jekyll Island a
massive twisted trunk still blocks
the path that leads into the
woods beyond.

Let's circumvent these long-dead
trunks that block our paths,
and wander deep
among the trees
along uncharted trails
in search of mysteries that
lie in wait for you
and me.

Two Walks

After an hour on the treadmill
I finished where I started…

After an hour on the path
I'm back where I departed…

Two walks that seemed
to lead nowhere do
not compare.

Unaware

Nurtured
by the sun and soil,
the rain and air,
we live
our lives
quite unaware
of nature's wondrous
synergies.

Uncertainty

We live hemmed-in between
time and eternity.

Just recently the wings of death
spread over our small town,
and took the lives of
two young men,
among our
brightest and our best.

Though death may
quell life's *sturm und drang,*
its joys and pains, its ups and downs,
who is to say we have to play
the game of zero sum?

So while in grief we
meet each day
confronted
by uncertainty, let
us embrace and celebrate
the way these moments blend
our lives into Eternity.

Urban Vision

After viewing Edward Hopper's <u>The Nighthawks</u>

An empty street curves round
a nighttime diner.

Inside, two large steel coffee urns
gleam in the diner's lights,
echoing silently
the pair
of nighthawks,
man and woman,
seated side-by-side on stools along the
curved lunch counter, drinking coffee late at night,
conversing with the white-capped waiter.

A third man sits alone,
preoccupied and lost in thought.

"What's going on," I wondered,
"What's happening?
Are they just waiting now for
someone to come, somewhere to go,
something to happen…hoping that Godot will
soon arrive and fill their lives without,
within, with meaning in this empty
urban wasteland?"

Voices from the Past

"Time holds us green and dying"
(Dylan Thomas)

–i–

After my father died I dreamed
we pitched a tent and
set up camp
beside a city street so
we could spend more time together.

Now after thirty years the sound
of his soft gentle voice still
echoes here inside.

–ii–

Like wisps of memory, the
voices from the past
now resonate
along the
corridors of our minds,
while time thus *holds us green and dying.*

Such inner voices bind us to our lives
like gentle ghosts that
hang around
until the time arrives
when we no longer need
to breathe them back to life again
in dreams and memories.

–iii–

Often our lives are richly blessed…
though sometimes cursed…
by voices from the past.

But we've been told such
voices are but coded memories
conveyed electrically within our brains,
transmitted cell to cell
synapse to synapse
until they reach
the switching station that
restores them once again as vivid
reminiscences from long ago,
awakening us
to what still lives
deep down within our souls.

So could it be Eternity may yet abide
within our souls, concealed
in dreams and
memories
while we yet live?

And after that, when we have died,
who knows?

Walnut Leaves

Though summer's barely gone,
the golden leaves from
walnut trees
descend in lazy swirls
many weeks before the white oaks
maples, basswoods, and our red bud trees
dispatch their leaves in flurries
to the ground.

Why must black walnut trees
leaf-out so late in spring,
and then release
their leaves
so soon,
while summer still
has glorious days to bring?

I think of narcissistic youths whose
beauty causes them to pause
and preen before
each mirror and windowpane.

Are they so full of *self* they
do not know their
outward show
will lose its glow,
and fade at summer's end?

Ah let them now enjoy the view...
for all too soon like leaves
on walnut trees
they will
begin to age,
and wonder where their
beauty's gone, and why they feel
so sad and very much alone
upon a summer's day.

Waterfall of Leaves

These brilliant autumn maple leaves...
bright red, orange, brown
dark green and gold...
recede
into the woods
as far as eye can see . . .
a watercolor still life, waiting there
in greater depth than I have ever seen.

Then suddenly a breeze
sets free a
waterfall of leaves...
a swirling blaze of colors
cascading down until they reach
their final resting place here
on this fertile ground.

Weavers

We are the weavers of the world,
seeking to create through
will and grace
our fate upon the earth.

Each day we send the shuttlecock of time
back and forth from side-to-side,
creating rich designs
upon our looms
as we reshape the
warp-and-woof of history
and try to stem the flow of falsehood
by embracing once again the timeless truths
we've known and cherished
through the years.

Web Designers

Let's not forget that ancient *Arachnids*
first designed "the web."

300 hundred million years ago
eight-legged spiders
sent forth coded
strands of
silky gossamer...
sticky, thread-like filaments
criss-crossing, circling,
forming complex
patterns
barely visible that
move and tremble in the breeze,
capturing tiny drops of dew that
sparkle in the sun like rare
and precious jewels.

And even now, today, she traps
and wraps her protein prey
inside her web...a meal
for another day.

Weeping Willow

A weeping willow tree with arms outstretched
sheltered the brook that ran through our
backyard...where almost every day
Karin and I would play,
building tiny dams
with sticks and stones to
change the water flow, and moving rocks
around to find the crawdads
hiding just below.

We learned to grab them quickly just
behind their two-armed pinchers
before they had a
chance to
turn around and
fight or scuttle off in flight.

Back then these tiny crabs seemed
just as fierce and frightening
as when, years later,
while camping
up in Maine, I reached into
a tank of large green lobsters
and selected one that later turned bright
orange, inside a pot of boiling water.

➘

As little children, when we
played beside that stream, the
pale green willow leaves o'erhead
held back the sun and rain,
and friendly branches
bending low
reached out to shelter us
beneath their leafy canopy...the
way an aging woman
bending low
protects her progeny.

What makes a poem?

More than
        rhetoric
                rhythm
                        rhyme
                a poet needs
                a song to sing . . .

        and if he finds
                he has no voice,
                        no song,
                                he tries
                        to bring forth
                from the void
        a fresh new melody
                by reaching,
                        breathing
                                deep within...
                and with the
        very breath of life
creating
        out of nothing
                a poem...
                        and a song.

↘

We're told
　　this is the way
　　　　it first was done,
　　　　　　long, long ago
　　　　when "in the beginning
　　　　was the Word . . ."
　　and from that Word,
a new Beginning.

When Dawn Doth Hover

Dawn doth hover at the break of day,
preparing for the moment
soon to be when
consciousness
will mount a fresh assault
upon our dream-filled state, with
sights and sounds that break apart the
deep, deep peace of last night's
wondrous sleep.

And now within
this wondrous space
between time and eternity
we lie awake, preparing for
another day.

Soon we'll cross dawn's threshold
and embrace the daily fray...
and when this day
comes to an end, we'll seek
some quiet time, before obliterating sleep
can claim us once again, and
loft us far away.

When I Take Her in My Arms

When we were young and green
'twas lover's heat that filled
our veins.

But when I take her
in my arms these days it's
not the same, for as we age,
embracing is more filled with
spirit, mind and soul
than passions
from our youth.

Now after all these many
years of memories
yet held dear
our love's become much
warmer, richer, deeper than
back then…and far
more blest.

While the Muse Doth Sleep

While the Muse doth sleep
I lie awake
communing with those
voices from the past...the
vast undying cloud of witnesses
that fills our lives each day
as we move forth into
an unknown
future, out along
the paths we daily tread,
in company with those still here...
the living, dying and
the dead.

Whose Life?

Some bishops have decreed they
need not heed our end-of-life
instructions to allow a
peaceful death
without unwanted interventions.

The new Directive overrides a
patient's written wishes by
insisting we receive
unwelcomed
impositions such as
heart pump stimulation,
artificial respiration, tubular nutrition,
even forced hydration . . .
unless (until) we're in
a final state of
active expiration from an
underlying cause or medical condition.

Such uninvited interventions by
certain institutions are
imposed
in spite of being
in a lasting vegetative state,
or comatose condition...even when
we've duly signed and posted in plain view
our DNR instructions that restate
our deep and final wish:
"Do Not Resuscitate!"

Wine and Roses

We miss the
days of wine and roses,
those gentler, softer years when
romance filled the air
in every season
against all reason...as now
upon the ground the
early springtime
flowers
spread 'round
their heady, rich perfume.

Winter Break

Will you not wait with me for
dawn to break?

The Puerto Rican roosters crow
their wake-up call and
all around
the sounds of
waking life resound.

We've come again you see to
Mary Lee's Beside-the-Sea,
to bask in Caribbean
light and take our
ease from winter's chill.

Here in this Paradise the morning sun
plays o'er the ocean waves
with tropical delight
while songbirds
fill the trees
with iridescent blaze
of colors, dazzling bright.

Each day the Bougainvillea open wide
and hummingbirds arrive to pollinate
and drink their fill from deep,
deep wells of nectar.

Across the open patio
cool breezes flow as silent
geckos scurry by and
climb the tiled
walls...
and high above
two circling predators
peer down upon their prey.

If you agree, let's stay until
the listless breath
of *ennui*
reminds us it is time
to join our friends and family
up north, among the silver maple trees.

Winter Solstice

During the longest night of every
year we seek the darkness
here inside that
germinates
new forms of life from seeds
of truth and beauty buried deep
within our souls.

So on this Solstice Day
we pray that fresh
epiphanies of
rarest roses
sharpest thorns will
blossom forth in wild and
riotous display, out of the fertile
rhizome of our souls.

Winter Thaw

Up north the frozen surface of our lake
lies bright and glistening
in the morning air,
as though a
million brilliant diamonds
had been spun and spread out
on the ice and snow.

Later, walking far off shore,
we felt a tiny crack
begin to open
underneath our feet,
then like a rifle shot explode
and race across the lake.

And in its wake
while we were rushing
for the safety of the shore
we heard a forlorn, haunting sound
that echoed round and round…it was
the hump-backed whale's
siren song of love.

Witchcraft?

Into these cauldrons deep within
we would-be poets pour
and blend our
longings, hopes,
doubts, and desires, our
thoughts, ideas, images and fears...
and slowly sift and stir the pot 'til
like a fabled witches' brew
alchemically
a fragrant stew soon
doth appear that hopefully will
satisfy you connoisseurs
of poetry.

Within Old Friends

Old friends so dear,
how we now
love the
sights and sounds,
the taste and touch and smell
of this most sensual, wondrous world!

And as we grow, year after year,
the world *within* is filled
with dreams and
hopes and memories
of things we did and hoped and
shared near every day
with you
and other families,
binding us all more deeply to the
fertile *rhizome of our souls...*
the deep down source
from which we all
draw love and
energy and truth that

↘

fills our lives with joy and happiness,
sadness and grace...until
life ends its warm
embrace.

Farewell, and *Namaste*.

Yesteryear

Our thoughts return to yesteryear
when out of the past
we hear
no thundering hooves
but only quiet echoes of the ones
we've known…and loved…and lost…
their voices calling, singing
laughing, prompting
asking, chiding
sharing
and supporting
one another, day by day
as we move further out along life's way…
empowered and enriched by
memories of their love.

About the Author

Born in 1933, the author earned degrees in music (Eastman), philosophy (Oberlin), and theology (Andover Newton), and served for a few years as a UCC minister. He went on to earn his Ph.D. in religion and literature at the University of Chicago and taught at Albion College for 28 years, then spent the next 14 years as a community volunteer.

In 2009 he and his wife moved to Silver Maples in Chelsea, where most of these poems were written.

When asked how he goes about writing poetry, Stohl said he had "no agenda or plan when starting a new poem, other than seeking to quiet the inconvenient urgings of his muse."

Address all inquiries to Dr. Johan Stohl, 1117 Silver Maples Drive, Chelsea, Michigan 48118 or contact him by email at yostohl@gmail.com